Ice Skating

by

Howard Bass

RAND McNALLY & COMPANY

Chicago · New York · San Francisco

Published in the U.S.A. by
Rand McNally & Company 1980.

© Grisewood & Dempsey Limited
1980.

Printed in the United States of America
by Rand McNally & Company.

SBN 528-82372-8

Library of Congress Catalog Card
No. 80-50304

Contents

Other books by the same author

The Sense in Sport
This Skating Age
The Magic of Skiing
Winter Sports
Success in Ice Skating
International Encyclopaedia
of Winter Sports
Let's Go Skating
Tackle Skating
Ice Skating for Pleasure

*Top left: The popular
Tai Babilonia and
Randy Gardner of the U.S.
giving one of their
stunning performances.*

*Left: John Curry of Great
Britain, the 1976 Olympic
men's champion, brought an
outstanding grace to men's
figure skating.*

*Top center: In his 'Scene on
the ice near a town',
Hendrik Avercamp presents
skating on the frozen Dutch
canals of his day.*

*Above: Ice hockey is one of
the fastest of all sports. It
can be one of the roughest
too.*

*Right: Soviet ice dancers,
Ludmila Pakhamova and
Aleksandr Gorshkov, in
Latin American mood.*

Foreword

Ice sports are marvellous! That's a fairly broad statement but with 43 years of involvement behind me, I have to admit I'm biased. I first went skating in 1936 and reached the giddy heights of participation in a dancing interval or two. I got my homework done early once a week to watch Brighton Tigers play their ice hockey matches. The only break was temporary, occasioned by World War II. On demobilization I went back to that same ice rink – the Sports Stadium in Brighton, England – and worked there. For twenty years.

I was privileged to make many friends in figure skating, ice hockey, speed skating, ice shows and among the writers. One such person is Howard Bass. I have known and respected his work for some 30 years now, and his high-standing reputation is universally acknowledged.

Howard has written many books on ice sports. This is the most comprehensive yet. It traces history. For the youngsters who may wish to perfect their sport, it tells them what to expect and how to cope. For the millions who watch ice sports on television it explains quite thoroughly those mystic terms unknown to the general viewer. And as a bonus it is without doubt the best illustrated work I have seen, both in pictorial and diagramatic form.

There is an ever-increasing desire for knowledge of these sports, probably due to presentation on television. But whether young beginner or armchair critic, no one could wish for a more informative volume encompassing every aspect of the wonderful world on ice.

Alan Weeks

Alan Weeks
BBC TV Commentator: Ice Skating and Ice Hockey
Director: Sports Aid Foundation.

The wide range of action possible on skates is emphasized by contrasting examples.
Previous page: Emi Watanabe, the American-based Japanese figure skater, gracefully negotiating an upright spin, adds a pleasing oriental flavor to her free skating. Her manner of presentation, with interpretation often timed to eastern-style music, gives an exotic touch to the championship's atmosphere.
Opposite: This elementary stag jump, simulating the leap of a deer, hardly taxes Britain's Robin Cousins, one of the world's outstanding exponents of jumps and spins.

Below: Speed, but still with elegance and economy of action, is epitomized by Eric Heiden, America's sensational world champion ice racer, here, cornering with consummate ease and an expression of happy self-assurance.

The Story of Skating

Not everyone understands the intricacies of skating on ice, but most enjoy what they see of it. That is why the whole family will gather round the television to watch a figure skating championship or an ice show.

The thrills and skills, grace and courage draw huge crowds to spacious indoor skating arenas. So commonplace has the modern ice stadium become that many skating stars have never performed on natural ice out of doors.

Archaeological evidence suggests that ice skating originated in northern Europe as long as two or three thousand years ago. It did not start as a sport or any kind of entertainment, but as a vital means of transportation. Earliest skates were crudely constructed from suitably sharpened shank or rib bones of the reindeer, ox or elk.

Skating as a sport began to develop from the 14th century, at first with simple races on frozen canals and rivers.

In 1742 the first skating club was formed in Edinburgh, Scotland, but it was not until 100 years later that the Skating Club of London was founded. Interest in pleasure skating soon began to spread to the United States and Canada. The first American club was formed in Philadelphia in 1849 and Canada's first organized rink opened in 1868.

New trends on the ice

An American named Jackson Haines, from Chicago, had successfully transposed to the ice some of his considerable knowledge of ballroom dancing. He popularized his new artistic skating technique during an extensive European tour beginning in 1864.

Thus far, all skating had been on natural ice in the open air. The first indoor rink with artificially frozen ice opened in Chelsea, south London, in 1876.

Right: Many artists of the sixteenth and seventeenth centuries depicted skating in their work, seizing on the colorful outdoor activity with its ideal contrasts of light and shade. Hendrik Avercamp included the sport in many Dutch scenes and this is a typical example of his observation of a day on the frozen canals of Holland, where early skating was so popular, recording for posterity the diversified fashions seen during the hard winters, which caused the ice-covered waterways to be used as near-normal shopping routes as well as for recreation. Other painters who favored skating scenes included Anthonie Beerstraaten, Pieter Brueghel, Cornelis Dusart and Isack van Ostade.

Below: Edwardian skating by lamplight in this scene at a well-attended carnival on ice on a frozen lake in one of London's parks (note the bandstand in the background). The ankle-length skirts must have greatly restricted skating, but warmth and convention of the time were overriding considerations.

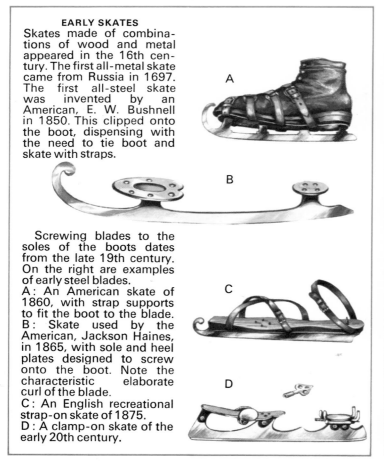

EARLY SKATES
Skates made of combinations of wood and metal appeared in the 16th century. The first all-metal skate came from Russia in 1697. The first all-steel skate was invented by an American, E. W. Bushnell in 1850. This clipped onto the boot, dispensing with the need to tie boot and skate with straps.

Screwing blades to the soles of the boots dates from the late 19th century. On the right are examples of early steel blades.
A: An American skate of 1860, with strap supports to fit the boot to the blade.
B: Skate used by the American, Jackson Haines, in 1865, with sole and heel plates designed to screw onto the boot. Note the characteristic elaborate curl of the blade.
C: An English recreational strap-on skate of 1875.
D: A clamp-on skate of the early 20th century.

Skating Associations

In 1879, the National Skating Association of Great Britain became the world's first administrative body in skating.

Other countries then began to form national associations of their own, beginning with the United States in 1886. The International Skating Union, with headquarters in Davos, Switzerland, was instituted in 1892. It now has 32 member nations.

Skating as an organized sport

The ISU has always been the governing body for both figure and speed skating. Both were among the earliest sports in the world to become properly organized for international competitions.

World speed skating championships for men officially date from 1893 and those for women from 1936. World figure skating championships began for men in 1896, for women in 1906, for pairs in 1908 and for ice dancing in 1952.

During the earliest years of the world figure championships, men and women competed in the same event. In 1902 Britain's Madge Syers narrowly missed claiming an early victory for women when she finished runner-up among her male opponents. She went on to win the first separate women's title at Davos in 1906.

Figure skating became the first ice or snow sport to gain Olympic status, with events for men, women and pairs forming part of the Summer Games in London in 1908, 16 years before the first separate Winter Olympics, in Chamonix, France, in 1924. Ice dancing was not added to the Olympic program until 1976.

Despite its rapid progress as a competitive sport, the advance of skating as a recreational pastime is slow today. More people are learning to skate then ever before, but there are not enough rinks to satisfy the mushrooming demand.

FAMOUS FIRSTS

The most world titles won by any figure skater is ten. Ulrich Salchow of Sweden, who invented one of the best known jumps, made his record with two straight runs of five, 1901-05 and 1907-11.

Sonja Henie of Norway, who achieved ten consecutive women's titles, 1927-36, afterwards became a skating film star (right).

Irina Rodnina, of USSR, won ten straight world pair titles with two partners, 1969-78.

The highest number of world ice dance victories has been six. Aleksandr Gorshkov and Ludmila Pakhomova, of USSR won them in 1970-74 and 1976.

The most difficult jump yet achieved is the triple axel. This involves three and a half mid-air rotations. The first to do it in an international competition was Vern Taylor of Canada, during the 1978 World Championships in Ottawa.

The first triple jump of all, a triple loop, was performed by Dick Button of the U.S. in 1947.

Above: A public session on an ice rink, with skaters at all levels of progress. A friendly helping hand is ever close and many new friendships begin through learning together. The beginner below has already learned to look straight ahead and not at his feet.

First Steps on the Ice

Learning to skate is as easy as learning to walk—or it would be if we began as early. But most of us have learned to walk long before visiting an ice rink, of course, so skating has to be more consciously learned.

When you go to the rink to skate for the first time the sight of competent performers can bother you. You may also feel nervous about falling on the ice and hurting yourself. But once you are actually wearing skates and out on the ice, you will start to concentrate on your rate of progress and forget your early fears.

The first thing to do when you get to the rink is go to its skate rental shop. There beginners can rent a pair of skates for a nominal charge per session. Just tell the attendant your normal shoe size.

How to start

Unless you already have a skating friend to help you, it is well worth paying for a few lessons. Go to the instructors' lesson desk at the rink, explain that you have not skated before and would like a junior instructor to keep an eye on you. A fifteen to twenty minute lesson at the outset is a worthwhile investment, because the professional can help you to gain confidence.

But you can easily go it alone if you prefer, by learning to balance on skates with the aid of the rink barrier. Avoid consciously lifting either skate from the ice. Think of the blades solely as gliders which move according to the degree of body weight transferred over each skate in turn.

You should attempt short glides only at first, and increase the length as your confidence grows.

No champion learns to skate without falling. And even the most experienced skater still falls occasionally. Learn to relax the muscles and not stiffen up when losing balance. Wear gloves to protect your hands. After a fall, do not rush to get up. Stay calm. First, kneel on one knee. Then, keeping your feet together, push your body up by pressing your hands on the ice in front and raising your skates to the toe points.

After two or three visits to the rink you will probably feel confident enough to leave the barrier.

WHAT TO AIM FOR

Not everyone who begins to skate starts out with a particular goal, but after a few weeks several ideas may occur. Many are content to be leisure-time skaters with neither the time nor the ambition to improve beyond simply skating for pleasure and exercise.

Others may be attracted to the social advantages of ice dancing. Then the best thing to do is join the rink's ice dance club and progress with other members. And budding racers may join the speed skating club.

Those who want a medal to prove their skating prowess must join their national skating association. This organizes all proficiency tests, from preliminary right through to bronze, silver and gold.

It is not possible to enter competitions or championships without first passing the appropriate test designed to prove a contestant's qualifying standard.

For those wishing to eventually earn a living from skating, two avenues are open: to become a professional coach or to join an ice show.

As a coach one must have a very thorough and critical knowledge of skating, and a high personal standard.

Theatrical skating producers are sometimes prepared to train someone with as little as two years' skating experience, provided that the right potential is apparent.

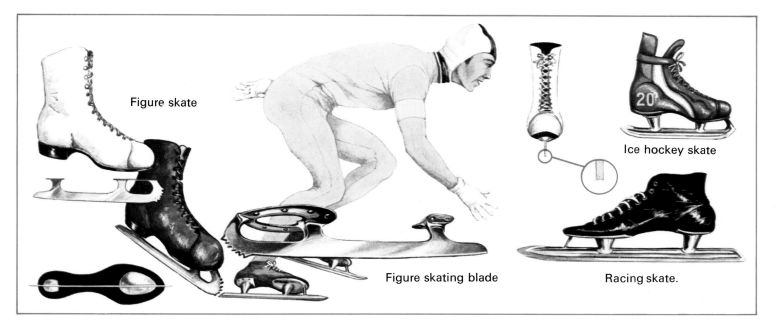

Figure skate

Ice hockey skate

Figure skating blade

Racing skate.

Looking at Skates

Above: Skates used for different purposes.

Below: Compared to the beginners, Robin Cousins makes a parallel spin look a sheer joy.

CARING FOR YOUR SKATES
When you have become accustomed to a pair of skates and boots, you will not want to part with them too soon, so taking care of them is important.

It is essential to protect the blades with skate guards when not in use. Always walk with the guards on between the changing room and the ice. This avoids blunting or damaging the blades on a wooden or concrete floor. It is normal to carry the guards when you are on the ice.

Always wipe the blades dry before putting them away and never leave them at a hot radiator, because the contrast in temperature could damage blade or boot.

Skate blades need to be sharpened after about 30 hours' actual skating. It is best to ask either the rink skate shop attendant or an experienced skater to recommend a really expert grinder because it is a specialized job.

Not everyone bothers to smear the blades with oil before putting them away or to fit trees or stuffed newspaper into the boots, but this does help to preserve them.

The boots should be kept clean by using a good quality cleaner which will not damage or dry out the leather. Special cleaners are available at most rink shops. In any case, few things look worse on the ice than dirty boots, which impress nobody—least of all competition judges.

There are three very distinctive kinds of ice skate: for figure skating (and all recreational skating), for speed skating and for ice hockey. Racing skates are not welcomed at public rink sessions because they encourage speed which, in turn, puts everyone at unnecessary risk.

The *figure skate* is made of chromium-plated steel and is hollow ground. This means that the underside of the blade is not flat, but has a groove right along its length, leaving two edges. Most figure skating movements are performed on one or other edge of the blade.

The width of the blade is just over 3mm ($\frac{1}{8}$in). It is only slightly longer than the boot. The figure blade is easily distinguishable from other skates by a series of saw-like teeth at the toe. These teeth are termed a toe-rake or toe-pick. They are designed to aid spinning and toe-assisted jumps.

The *racing skate* is notably longer, sometimes exceeding 450mm (18in) and has a thinner blade. The racing boot has lower ankle supports and so looks more like a shoe.

The *ice hockey skate* is of roughly similar length to that used for figures and recreational skating, but it differs in other respects. It has a plain, pointed end and is about half the thickness of the figure blade. The blade is reinforced with hollow tubing.

The hockey skate (except that used by the goaltender) also has a lower ankle support than the figure boot and stands higher from the ice. The hockey boot has reinforced caps at toe and heel and is made of extra thick material to protect the player from possible damage during the action of a game.

In all cases, the blade of the skate is attached to metal sole-plates fitted with holes, through which screws fix it to the sole of the boot.

Skates and boots are either sold separately or as sets already fitted together. The beginner or advanced performer is likely to purchase a set, but the more experienced skater usually prefers to buy the boot separately and have favorite blades attached.

13

Forwards and Backwards

The beginner learns how to skate forwards more quickly by taking very short strokes at first, without lifting the disengaged skate much. The essence of the action is to put the weight (that is, the shoulder) over the blade making the stroke, on an outside edge.

You should maintain an upright posture, with eyes focused ahead in the direction of travel, not looking down at the feet. Each stroke takes you outwards rather than in a straight line. Provided the knees are bent at the start of each stroke, with arms held waist-high and palms downwards, you can control longer strides.

Moving backwards

Skating backwards takes more time and patience. Again, the knee of the skating foot must be bent. The most common error is to lean forwards during this backward-moving action. The body weight still has to be kept over the skating leg, but this means that the body must not lean backwards to go backwards.

Another fault is to look down at the ice instead of looking over the shoulder in the direction of travel. Early correction of these initial mistakes makes progress much quicker.

Cornering

The art of comfortable cornering is acquired by mastering the crossover. This is an action in which one foot crosses over the other to give smooth continuity while changing direction. There is a greater feeling of the blade's edge, and a sense of balancing at an angle while turning, rather like that experienced when biking around a curve.

Above: The correct forward action. The skating knee is slightly bent and the free leg held out behind to assist balance. The body weight is poised forward over the skating foot. The eyes are looking straight ahead and not down. The arms are held out on either side, with palms downward and waist-high.

Above: Skating backwards. At first it is best to move without lifting either skate from the ice, to learn the correct positioning of body weight over the skating foot. The action is effected by pushing from the inside of the blade. Note the well-bent knees and the need to keep erect, to offset the tendency to fall forward. Once under way, the skater looks over the shoulder in the direction of travel.

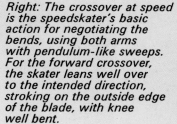

Left: Preparing to corner with a crossover movement, wherein one foot crosses over the other to facilitate smooth continuation in a curving direction.

Right: The crossover at speed is the speedskater's basic action for negotiating the bends, using both arms with pendulum-like sweeps. For the forward crossover, the skater leans well over to the intended direction, stroking on the outside edge of the blade, with knee well bent.

Stopping

Once you have learned the basic technique of skating forwards, you can gather speed with ease and feel relaxed until, with a barrier rushing up at you or a prostrate figure in your path, you may suddenly realize that you have not the faintest idea how to stop in a hurry – and the result is an inelegant panic fall.

So it is prudent to learn at least one way to put the brake on as soon as you are able to skate forwards.

Some stopping techniques

The abrupt stop that produces a spectacular shower of ice flakes is called the *skid stop,* and is frequently used by ice hockey players. It is too difficult a method for the beginner to learn at first.

The easiest method is the *T-stop.* It is a simple process of touching the non-skating blade lightly on the ice behind the skating blade. The two skates are thus in the shape of the letter T. The same result can be achieved by putting the non-skating blade in front of the other. The movement has to be smooth, not sudden.

An alternative method for the more experienced skater is the *snowplow* or *arrowhead stop.* This is achieved by bringing both skates together to glide parallel, before forcing the heels outwards (keeping the toes of the skates about half a foot's length apart). The action is similar to the snowplow in skiing: bending the knees while inclining each blade on its inside edge.

The more advanced *skid* or *hockey stop* is accomplished by quarter-turning both feet sideways, bending the knees and counter-rotating the body at the last moment. This maneuver is strictly for the seasoned performer.

When skating backwards, you can stop by raising the heels of both skating blades simultaneously. This should first be practiced with one foot at a time. The important thing is to lean well forward, away from the direction of travel, to avoid falling backwards.

Left: The fundamental T-stop used by beginners for coming to a halt. The inside edge of the non-skating blade is dragged gently on the ice just behind the heel of the skating blade.

Right: The snowplow stop, as in skiing, with feet in arrowhead formation, inclining both blades on inside edges.

Below: Robin Cousins braking with legs apart, more difficult than when together.

Right: The more difficult skid or "hockey" stop is effected by quarter-turning both skates sideways, producing a skid by pressure on the sides of each blade.

International School Figures

There are 41 school figures in the international schedule, each consisting of two or three lobes. Their object is to teach and test the skater's ability to trace circles smoothly and steadily.

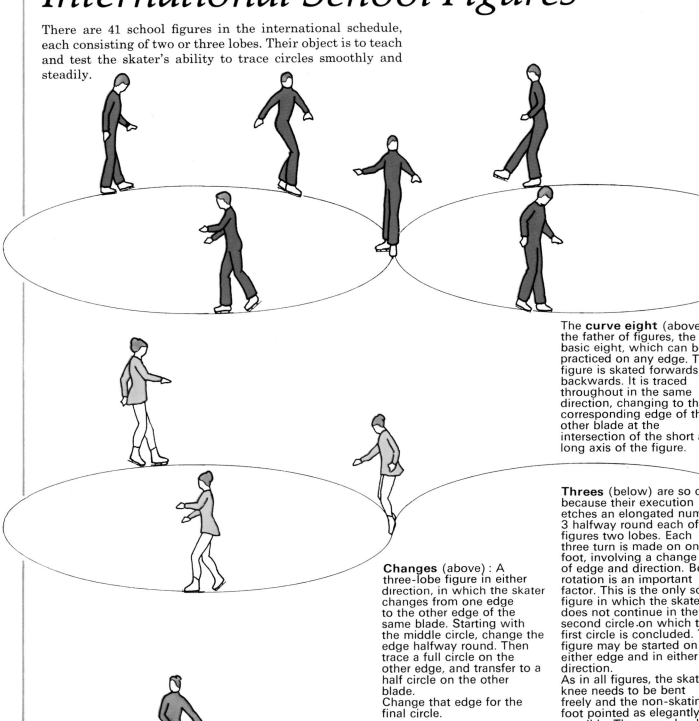

The **curve eight** (above) is the father of figures, the basic eight, which can be practiced on any edge. The figure is skated forwards or backwards. It is traced throughout in the same direction, changing to the corresponding edge of the other blade at the intersection of the short and long axis of the figure.

Threes (below) are so called because their execution etches an elongated numeral 3 halfway round each of the figures two lobes. Each three turn is made on one foot, involving a change of edge and direction. Body rotation is an important factor. This is the only school figure in which the skater does not continue in the second circle on which the first circle is concluded. The figure may be started on either edge and in either direction.

As in all figures, the skating knee needs to be bent freely and the non-skating foot pointed as elegantly as possible. The arms should be held out about waist-high to balance, with palms downwards. Each stroke has to be smooth and deliberate, without jerking.

Changes (above): A three-lobe figure in either direction, in which the skater changes from one edge to the other edge of the same blade. Starting with the middle circle, change the edge halfway round. Then trace a full circle on the other edge, and transfer to a half circle on the other blade.
Change that edge for the final circle.

16

The **double three** (right) involves two consecutive three turns in each circle of a two lobe figure. The threes are executed at third-way distances round each circle. Because each turn reverses direction, the skater ends each circle on the same edge and in the same direction as when starting it. The skater starts the second circle on the other foot.

The **loop** (above) is a two-lobe figure in which an eclipse is traced within each circle. Both circle and elipse (loop) are skated on the same foot and on the same continuous edge, with no break between them. The second circle is traced on the corresponding edge of the opposite foot as that used for the first, and in the same direction. Ideally, the diameter of the circle should be about equal to the skater's height (say 5 feet, about 1.5 meters) each loop one-third the total length of the circle. This figure has to be skated at a controlled speed.

The **bracket** (below) is a two-lobed figure, leaving a tracing similar to a three, except that the turn mark on the far end of each circle points outwards (opposite to a three tracing). The bracket itself is a half-turn executed halfway round each circle, involving a change of edge and direction on the same blade. The body turns inside the circle, and both edges in the turn are forced opposite to the natural curve of the edge. Each circle is skated on a different foot.

The **rocker** (below) is a three-lobe figure featuring the rocker turn, in which the skater appears to begin a three turn, but there is no change of edge at the point of the turn. Instead, the skate rotates sufficiently to come out of the turn on the same edge, but in different direction.

The ability to maintain a true and steady curve in compulsory figures is dependent on a correct start from 'rest',—a strong but controlled push-off from the center of the figure to be traced.

The three-lobe **counter** (above) tests the ability to perform the counter half-turn, which is entered as when performing a bracket, but exited as when performing a three, causing a change of direction but maintaining the same edge before and after the turn.

Important factors for the skater to remember, as in all figures, is to keep the weight of the body as much as possible over the skating foot; to press the skating hip in towards the center of the body, holding it motionless at all times; and to prevent the hips from rotating in the direction of the circle rotation.

The **change double three** (above) of three lobes incorporates the technique of changing edge and tracing double threes in the same figure.

Below: A demonstration of paragraph loops, showing the actual tracings on the ice, performed by Christopher Howarth, who shortly after was runner up in the British championships.

The **change loop** figure (left and below), also three lobes, involves changing edges and tracing loops.

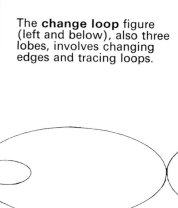

Spins and Jumps

SPINS AND JUMPS

Spins should be performed as nearly as possible on one spot, without "travelling". It is important to hold the head high at the beginning of the spin. To gather momentum, the arms are pulled in gradually, until they are held close to the body. To stop, the free foot is taken away slowly from the skating foot as speed slackens, and touched on the ice with the toe-pick to check momentum.

The arms are opened out at the same time to check the shoulder rotation.

A sit spin is performed by positioning one leg in front of the other and squatting down into the spin. A camel spin (left) is achieved by raising one leg behind and lowering the torso parallel to the ice.

Right: Denise Biellmann of Switzerland in a catch hold spin, an upright spin in which the skater reaches over and grabs hold of the raised skate.

Far left: Like all pair skaters, Marina Tcherkasova (USSR) performs similar movements to those of a soloist when "shadow" skating in partnership. Here, she is seen turning in the air during an axel jump.

The **salchow** jumper (below) begins with a forward outside three to turn onto a right back inside edge, taking off from that edge. He turns counter-clockwise in the air before landing on the left back outside edge of the other skate. Height is more important than distance.

Left: The **axel** jumper takes off from a forward outside edge with the free leg coming through, and makes one-and-a-half mid-air counter-clockwise rotations before landing on a left back outside edge of the other skate.

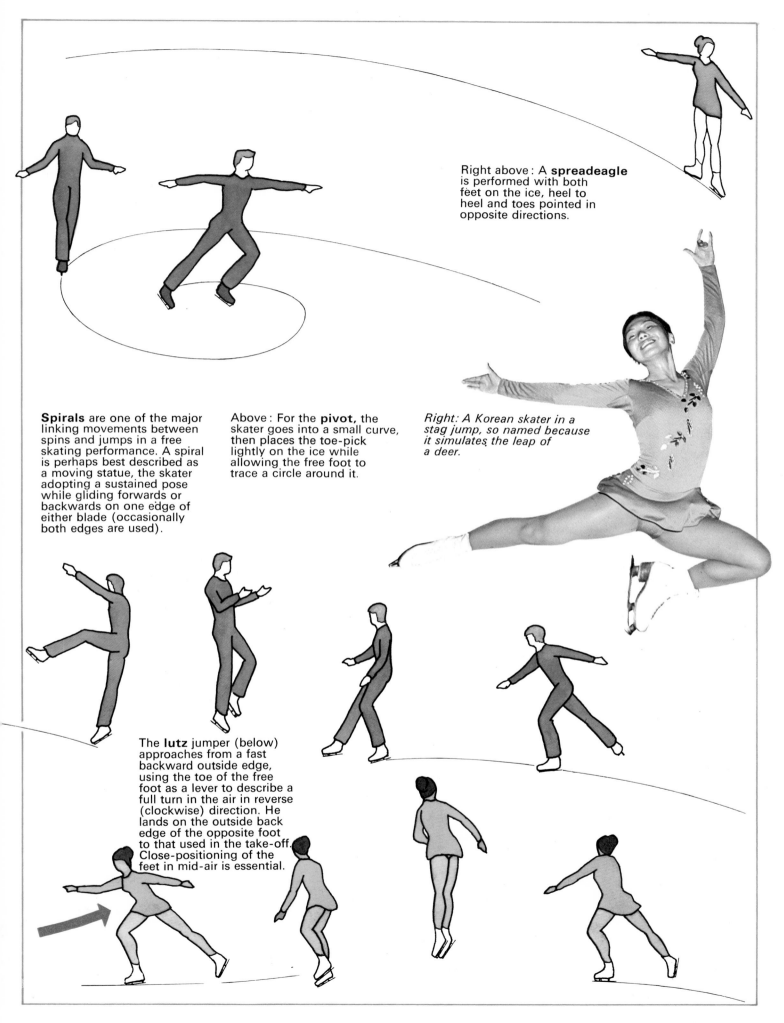

Right above: A **spreadeagle** is performed with both feet on the ice, heel to heel and toes pointed in opposite directions.

Spirals are one of the major linking movements between spins and jumps in a free skating performance. A spiral is perhaps best described as a moving statue, the skater adopting a sustained pose while gliding forwards or backwards on one edge of either blade (occasionally both edges are used).

Above: For the **pivot,** the skater goes into a small curve, then places the toe-pick lightly on the ice while allowing the free foot to trace a circle around it.

Right: A Korean skater in a stag jump, so named because it simulates the leap of a deer.

The **lutz** jumper (below) approaches from a fast backward outside edge, using the toe of the free foot as a lever to describe a full turn in the air in reverse (clockwise) direction. He lands on the outside back edge of the opposite foot to that used in the take-off. Close-positioning of the feet in mid-air is essential.

Pair Skating

Of all the competitions in the figure skating championships, pair skating is probably the most exacting and physically demanding. Each partner is so dependent on the other and their perfect understanding and smooth cohesion are basic essentials for success.

Left: When starting to skate together the pair skate side by side. The man has his right arm around his partner's waist. She has her left arm around him. They hold each other's hands in front. This position gives support and helps coordination. The pair then learn to skate both forward and backward, matching their movements as nearly as possible. To achieve this, each stroke needs to match in length, depth of edge and bend of knee. The movements of each head and body should be as one. Pair skaters are aiming to skate like a single figure.

There is no basic hold in pair skating to compare with that in ice dancing.
Left: The Americans, Randy Gardner and Tai Babilonia, about to enter a death spiral. The man has a firm left-hand hold on his partner's left hand, an all-important grip that will guide her throughout the movement as she spirals round his rotating body, gradually lowering and bending hers backwards until her hair brushes the ice. This is perhaps the most important pairs movement while in bodily contact, apart from overhead lifts.

Above: When skating together, partners **shadow** each other, each enacting the same movement simultaneously as if one were the shadow of the other. Unlike the soloist, a pair skater has to learn not only how to perform a spin or jump well, but to do so in perfect harmony with the same movement by the partner. They are not obliged always to perform identical moves while separated, however, so long as their actions give a homogeneous impression.

Left: Separating to perform in harmony, each pair skater will accomplish solo spins, jumps and double jumps—even triple jumps if both are capable—of a standard equal to soloists.

It is thus easy to imagine that many a top pair skater might well have become a distinguished solo performer instead, had he or she concentrated exclusively on single skating.

Above: Lifts form the spectacular highlights of pair skating achievements, depending so much on timing, on the man's strength when holding his partner aloft, and on the girl's ability to fulfil mid-air requirements.
Here, the pair perform a **three jump lift.** As the woman springs upwards, her partner pushes upwards with his left arm to assist her jump. They continue together along the same curve after the jump.

Above right: Moving together when in bodily contact, pair skaters endeavor to perform as an entity. In pair spins, they rotate in perfect harmony. Even during spirals, they move together as if one person. This skill is the result of a deep understanding born probably of many years' arduous practice together. The need for their matching technical standards and off-ice compatibility is a sternly tested and vital ingredient.

Right: This move demonstrates the dependance of one skater on the other in a pair partnership. The male partner is usually quite a bit taller than his partner, which is a helpful factor in a lift like this.

Strict limits to lifts are imposed in ice dancing, but the six-times Soviet world champions, Aleksandr Gorshkov and Ludmila Pakhomova, knew how to make them artistic. In competitions, the dancing "mini lift" must not exceed one and a half revolutions and the man must not lift his partner above waist height, but in exhibitions ice dancers have a chance to be more spectacularly athletic and sometimes attempt a few moves more familiar to pair skating.

Skating Together

Left: Randy and Tai, who demonstrate lifts so well, show here an example of the man's perfect control and need for great strength. An injury to Randy's leg, which would have jeopardized Tai, forced their withdrawal from the 1980 Olympics. Expectations were high and the decision a painful one, not only for the pair but for their fans.

Below: Rolf Oesterreich and Romy Kermer, of East Germany were twice the closest challengers to the Soviet world champions, Aleksandr Zaitsev and Irina Rodnina, when the latter were at the peak of their career. Rolf and Romy gained world silver medals in 1975 and 1976 after finishing third in 1974. They were also runners-up in the Olympic pairs event at Innsbruck in 1976. Here, they shadow each other in a pair sit spin.

CHOOSING A PARTNER

Skaters are usually suggested as suitable partners by an instructor prepared to coach them. Several factors have to be considered before a pair embark on a course of preparation together. If the right selection is not made at the outset, a lot of ice time can be wasted.

If both partners are of a similar standard, neither will slow down the other's progress.

They should start young and, ideally, the boy ought to be several inches taller. He must be strong enough to lift the girl and she must be light enough to be lifted.

The two may be in each others' company for years, both on and off the ice, so similar interests and temperaments are advantageous.

Pair skating is a highly specialized form of the sport. It involves many movements, such as lifts, which only pairs can do. But it also includes the jumps, spins and spirals which soloists perform, but which have to be done in harmony by a pair.

A pair will plan their performance so that it contains a constant variation between the elements they can only do while in physical contact and those for which they skate separately.

The best known movements with the pair in contact are the death spiral and the pair sit spin, and a series of lifts including the overhead axel lift, the lasso lift, the split lutz lift, and the twist lift. Pair skaters can also perform spectacular throw movements.

The pair can also skate apart and at a distance from one another. The term for this form of pair skating is shadow skating. The idea here is for the pair to jump or spin simultaneously and harmoniously. They need not necessarily perform identical moves, but they must blend their actions suitably.

All pair movements must have the emphasis on skating, as distinct from feats of strength or other skills more in keeping with a variety act. For example, lifts must be carried out with a continuous motion of ascent and descent. The man may not otherwise hold his partner overhead; he cannot swing her horizontally through the air and must not hold her by the leg or neck.

In senior championships, each pair has first what is called a short program, during which six specified elements have to be performed within two minutes. This effort is worth a quarter of the total marks; the rest are awarded for the long free program, for which each couple has to put together a five-minute program.

Right: Randy and Tai, showmen to the last, take their bows at the end of their performance.
In Vienna in 1979, Randy Gardner and Tai Babilonia became America's first pair skating champions of the world in 29 years. Both members of the Los Angeles Figure Skating Club, they are coached in California by Britain's John Nicks, who himself won the world title in 1953 with his sister, Jenny. Randy and Tai began skating at the ages of nine and seven respectively. Randy is the senior by two years and, in 1974, when they were only 15 and 13, they became the youngest pair ever to represent the United States in world competition. Each became an accomplished soloist before they concentrated exclusively on pair work.

Left: When skating together a pair, as here, will harmonize their dress as well as their movements.

Below: March 29, 1979, was an historic day for British skating, when a truly royal ice gala, attended by Queen Elizabeth and the Duke of Edinburgh, was held at Wembley Arena to mark the centenary of the National Skating Association of Great Britain.

All the medallists from the world championships, held in Vienna earlier the same month, skated exhibitions, as did John Curry, the 1976 triple crown winner of the world, Olympic and European titles.

Every former British world champion was invited to be presented to Her Majesty and to receive a special commemorative medal. Here, Tai Babilonia is being presented to the Queen. On Tai's left is her partner, Randy Gardner, with John Curry next to him.

25

Preparing a Program

A free skating performance in a senior championship lasts five minutes for men or pairs, four for women or ice dance couples. The participant's task is to arrange the best movements they can and link them together in an order that will provide plenty of variation, minimum repetition and smooth continuity.

The program has to be planned so that the interest of the judges and spectators is sustained throughout. If an onlooker's mind starts wandering during a skater's performance, it means the program lacks variety and interest. The element of surprise should be considered and items that are original and different should be included where possible.

The whole rink area should be used intelligently, so that highlights are evenly distributed in different parts of it. Some maneuvers, like a split jump, are best performed near the center because of the spectacular effect, but spins or spreadeagles can be just as effective at either end. Care must also be taken not to plan anything too close to the barrier, because this will not allow for any slight miscalculations.

Varying pace

The skater must also consider stamina, and pace the program accordingly. Rigorous movements should be

CHOOSING MUSIC

With knowledge of the kind of technical program intended, the skater seeks suitable music to accompany it. This is in no sense background music. It must be of appropriate tempo, with pronounced beats to which the landings of jumps may be timed. It should express the kind of mood the skater wishes to portray, and so enhance the performance.

The right selection properly interpreted can make all the difference to the presentation. A skater has to use the music to personal advantage. Very often, a single melody is not in itself descriptive enough for all the actions the skater plans to perform, so two or three pieces have to be joined. This has to be done carefully, so that it will not offend the musical ear.

performed when fresh, with more gentle and graceful moves timed for periods of breathlessness.

Judges give extra marks for difficult techniques well done, so the higher the level that can be achieved without error the better. A competitor knows a triple jump will earn more than a double, and anyone who can include several without undue risk will always do so. On the other hand, a fault or a fall will be penalized, so 'if in doubt, leave it out' is sometimes a good rule unless one is determined in trying for a make-or-break effort.

It is important not to crowd too many similar actions together, except perhaps to demonstrate the ability to present a special combination or series of jumps. A good jumper is sometimes apt to forget that other elements need to be included. In any case, trying to pack in too many jumps, however difficult and well executed, can make the performance look monotonous and will not show a skater's versatility.

Despite the hazards, the tension and the butterflies in the stomach, a contestant has to look cheerful and confident.

A happy expression suggests, and indeed helps, confidence; a studious one implies anxiety.

How the judges decide

Competitors are assessed not only for what they do but for how they do it. The judges award two sets of marks: the first are for technical merit, and the second for artistic presentation. So a skater who makes a technical error may be marked lower because of it in the first set, but may not be penalized in the second, if the general performance was not at fault.

Finally, the whole program has to be timed to music of the competitor's choice. The skater who really uses the music well, who times jumps precisely to the beat and interprets the mood, is bound to have extra impact.

Certain pieces of music have become favorites with top skating stars and so have been recorded to their tempo. There are some records made specially for skating, which will probably include such music as the *Light Cavalry Overture, Carmen* and *The Dream of Olwen,* all of which have proved to be popular choices with top skaters, or one can of course choose one's own musical program.

Left: Performing a simple stag jump is Linda Fratianne, the petite American who won the world women's title in 1977, losing it narrowly the next year to the East German, Anett Pötzsch, but regaining it from her in 1979. She is coached by Frank Carroll in Los Angeles.

Below: Another great American skater was Dorothy Hamill, world and Olympic champion in 1976. Her speciality was a camel jump-spin which became dubbed the "Hamill camel", pictured here. A skater who can introduce such spectacular movements into a program, and perform

them flawlessly, becomes a star. Dorothy was twice world runner-up in the two seasons before gaining the title. Having achieved the crown, she capitalized on it by turning professional and delighting U.S. televiewers with her own spectacular brand of show skating.

Left: Charlie Tickner gained the world men's title for the United States in Ottawa in 1978, defeating Jan Hoffman, the East German runner-up, and third-placed Britain's Robin Cousins in probably the closest to a triple tie the sport will ever know. A powerful jumper with a fine repertoire of triples, Charlie is trained by Norma Sahlin in Denver, Colorado.

Ice Dancing

Dancing on skates has been practiced for well over 300 years, and the diarist Samuel Pepys claimed to have danced on the ice with Nell Gwynne when the Thames froze in 1683. Ice dancing became popular in Vienna in the late 19th century, but it was the English who turned it into a competitive sport. The British championships began in 1937, though world championships did not start until 1952 and ice dancing was not included in the Olympic Games until 1976. So, in the championship arena at least, it is a much newer event than figure skating.

Competition dancing

When the world championships began, British skaters were far ahead of those from other countries because they had been dancing in competitions for longer. Most of the dances had been invented in London and had been practiced there since the 1930s. So Britain won the world title for nine years in succession. After 1960, however, fortunes began to change.

Ice dancing has the same sort of social attraction as ballroom dancing, and so far more people choose to do that rather than pair skating. The competition for championships is therefore intense.

For international events, 12 specific dances are recognized, and three of these are included each season in the compulsory dance sections of the world championships. They include four waltz variations—the Viennese waltz, the Westminster waltz, the starlight waltz, and the Ravensburgher waltz. Of different moods, style and tempo are the blues, the paso doble, the quickstep, and the rhumba.

Above: Warren Maxwell and Janet Thompson, the British ice dancers who, in 1977, came closest to breaking a Soviet monopoly of the world title which has lasted since 1970. They were impressive runners-up, but a subsequent leg injury sustained by Janet retarded their future progress. They are particularly remembered for well synchronized free leg actions.

Aleksandr Gorshkov and Ludmila Pakhomova won the world dance title for USSR a record six times and, in 1976, became the first Olympic gold dance medallists. Whether in classical mood (right) or (as at the top of the facing page) in a flippant Latin-American mood, their smooth-flowing steps and musical interpretation were widely admired.

DANCERS OR PAIRS
The layman watching ice dancing for the first time may ask: what is the difference between ice dancing and pair skating?

Pair skating is a much more rigorous event. One partner may be lifted above the other's head, or even thrown through the air from a jump. Lifts and jumps of this kind are not allowed in ice dancing.

Everything an ice dancer does must conform with a recognized ice dance characteristic and be part of a genuine dance sequence, however original.

There are strict limitations as to what a couple may do in a competition. Only small lifts are allowed, which means that the man may not raise his hands above his waist, and lifts may not exceed $1\frac{1}{2}$ revolutions.

Jumps, for changing foot or direction, may not exceed $1\frac{1}{2}$ rotations.

Separations should not last longer than 5 seconds, except for an 8-second one in the first sequence. Time for arabesques and pivots is also limited.

These are familiar ballroom dances, unlike the kilian, which is skated to march rhythm. The other three dances are the yankee polka, tango romantica and Argentine tango.

For the basic waltz position, the man's right hand holds his partner between the shoulder blades. Her left hand rests slightly below the man's right shoulder and her left elbow rests on his right elbow. The man's left arm and his partner's right one are extended with hands held firmly to make correct movement easier.

The kilian is quite different. Instead of facing one another, the partners face in the same direction. They stand side by side, the girl on her partner's right, with his right shoulder behind her left shoulder. Her left arm stretches in front of her partner's chest, and they hold each other's left hands. His right arm goes behind her back, so that their right hands are clasped at her waist, just above the hip bone.

The dance program

The three compulsory dances in a championship, with standard music for all competitors, are together worth 30 per cent of the total marks. They are followed by what is called a set pattern dance. This is danced to a recognized pattern on the ice and to a specified rhythm, announced at the beginning of the season, which may be waltz, march, tango or whatever. Within these limits, the dancers can create their own performance and select their own music. The set pattern dance is worth another 20 per cent of the marks.

The remaining 50 per cent is awarded for the final section of the event, the free dancing. This lasts four minutes for each couple, and allows the dancers to devise any kind of dance routine they like, within recognized dance regulations. They may change the dance and the tempo during the performance, and can choose any music. This is a challenge to creative skill, and is the most popular part of the contest.

Below and right: Andrei Minenkov and Irina Moiseeva, another great Russian dance couple known to millions of televiewers as 'Min and Mo', won the world title twice, in 1975 and 1977.

Above: Racers race in pairs against the clock, rather than each other. Each pair changes lanes once every lap, so that both cover the same distance.

Below: Fritz Schaly of the Netherlands, wearing the modern, close-fitting catsuit style of clothing now preferred because of its streamlined wind-resisting effect. The race starter is seen to the left behind him.

Speed Skating

Speed skating is the oldest form of competition on ice blades. The instinct to go faster than someone else is a more natural urge than the more intricate, artistic aspect of the sport which developed later. Racing began in the Netherlands in the 17th century, and the Dutch introduced it to the English Fens in about 1814. World championships for men have been officially recognized from 1896. Women's titles were first contested in 1906. Olympic events for men date from 1924 and for women from 1960.

There are four men's and four women's world events. The men's are 500, 1500, 5000 and 10,000 meters. The women's are 500, 1000, 1500 and 3000 meters. The world title goes to the racer with the best overall performance in all four distances, worked out on a points basis. Individual distance winners do not gain official titles.

The Olympic system is different. There is no overall champion, but medals and titles are awarded to the winners over each distance. The race distances are the same as for world events but there is also a 1000-meter event for men.

The circuit and its use

The standard international circuit is oval and is 400 meters long. It consists of two tracks. Competitors are drawn to race in pairs, but they race against the clock rather than against each other. They must stay in their own tracks, except when interchanging once every lap. This is done during a clearly marked stretch along one of the straights. The racer moving in from the outer track is responsible for avoiding a collision. If officials agree that a racer is balked during the changeover, they can allow that racer a re-run.

The style is impressive. Racers take long strides while maintaining a crouched position, and often cover the straights with both hands clasped behind the back, to lessen wind resistance and increase stamina. They always race

Above: Marathon speed skating is very popular in Holland, with pack-style racing instead of the more familiar two-at-a-time system used in international championships.

Below: The length of speed skates are clearly shown here; Leah Poulos, one of the recent bevy of crack American women sprinters, won a silver Olympic medal for the 1000 meters at Innsbruck in 1976

counter-clockwise and, when cornering, the right hand swings like a pendulum to help speed and balance.

Speed skating equipment

Skin-hugging catsuits and protective woolen headgear are the normal attire for ice racing. The speed skating blades are longer than those used for figure skating, and are usually about 425 mm (17 in). The blade is also much thinner, but still has two edges. The footwear is more like a shoe than a boot, lower at the ankle and made of thin, lightweight leather.

The most successful racers come, in the main, from Norway, Netherlands, the United States, Sweden, and the USSR. The Scandinavians and Dutch have a reputation for following their favorite racers, rather like football crowds and in comparable numbers. Ice racing was a major national sport in Norway and Sweden long before the days of electrical refrigeration, and the Dutch have been devotees of the sport since they began to race on their frozen canals centuries ago.

The size of racing circuits means that they have to be outdoors, and they are costly to maintain – championship tracks are all artificially frozen nowadays. Consequently, the number of tracks is limited and many aspiring racers do not live near one.

These skaters are faced with two alternatives – to make arrangements to live near an outdoor circuit for at least three months of the year if world championship skating is their goal, or to be content with indoor speed skating.

Indoor speed skating is called short track racing because the standard track for this is only 110 meters long. The distances used for short track championships are 500, 1000, 1500 and 3000 meters for both men's and women's events.

Ice Hockey

Ice hockey is the fastest team game there is. Because of the rapid action, the players have to be changed often, to avoid fatigue and to cool tempers. The fast tempo is increased by the electrical timing of play. The clock stops whenever the puck is not moving. A match comprises three 20-minute periods of actual play.

The game is an offshoot of field hockey and the first recorded game was in 1860, on the frozen Canadian harbors of Kingston, Ontario.

Equipment and clothing

The puck is disc-shaped, 25 mm (1 in) thick and 75 mm (3 in) in diameter, and is made of vulcanized rubber. The laminated wooden stick has a straight blade, which must be no longer than 37 cm (14½ in). The handle length must not exceed 135 cm (53 in). The angle (lie) of the blade and handle varies according to a player's personal choice. Some people prefer a more slanting angle, which means striking the puck when it is further away from the body.

The skate blade is 1.5 mm ($\frac{1}{16}$ in) wide and is slightly longer than the sole of the boot, but shorter than the speed skate. The blade is fitted to strong but lightweight hollow tubing. The boot has lower ankle supports than the figure skating boot, rising to about 125 mm (5 in) above the sole. The boot has reinforced caps at heel and toe, tendon protectors and molded arch supports.

Players are protected by pads on knees and elbows, guards on shins and shoulders, thick gauntlets and extra long socks under their shorts and sweaters, which are in their team colors. Helmets are optional.

The goaltender's equipment is more specialized. He is allowed extra-large leg-guards and odd gloves, one for holding the stick and the other for catching the puck. The metal stanchions, which connect skate to boot, are lower for better balance and maneuverability, and patterned so that there is no slot through which the puck can pass between the skate blade and boot sole. Goaltenders are also allowed to wear face masks, and may wear helmets.

The ice hockey rink

The maximum size of rink area for international matches is 61 m (200 ft) long by 30 m (98 ft) wide. The rink is bordered

Above: International ice hockey at its best is usually on the cards when the Soviet national team is involved, and rivalry can hardly be keener than when the United States (in white) provides the opposition. In these pictures, taken during the 1976 Innsbruck Olympics, the referee (in striped shirt) is wisely vigilant.

Above right: A United States forward and a Russian defender chase a loose puck. The protective helmets and the well padded apparel, including pads at knee, elbow and shoulder protect players against the dangers of a carelessly wielded stick or a crash onto the ice or into the barrier.

SUMMARY OF RULES

When the puck is outside a team's defense zone, only three defenders may stay within it. A player must not enter the attacking zone ahead of the puck. A pass must not be accepted from a team mate who, at the time of passing, is in another zone. In other words, a player can stay onside only by passing to a colleague in the same zone, or to anyone in his own half if he is in his defense zone.

Players infringing the rules are penalized by serving time in a penalty box, commonly called the 'sin bin'. A two-minute banishment is imposed for charging, elbowing, tripping, body-checking, high sticks or deliberately hitting out of the rink.

A penalty of five minutes is given for fighting and 10 minutes for serious misconduct or abusive language. A player can be sent off for the rest of the game (a match penalty) in extreme cases.

A team has to play on with five or fewer players on the ice when it has one or more players in the box, but a goalie's penalty may be served by a nominated team colleague, and substitutes are permitted for both teams when each has a player serving a penalty simultaneously.

A player may catch or stop the puck with his hand or any part of the body, so long as it is not held for more than three seconds and not propelled forward except by the stick or skate. A goal may be scored only from the stick and not while an attacking player is within the goal crease.

The international game is controlled by two referees. Professional matches have a referee and two linesmen.

all round by a barrier, up to 122 cm (4 ft) high, curved at each of the four corners. The red goal lines at each end are 4 m (13 ft) from the barrier and play may continue behind the goal line. The goals are 183 cm (6 ft) wide and 122 cm (4 ft) high, with nets not less than 60 cm (2 ft) deep. Two blue lines divide the rink into three equal zones (attacking, neutral and defending) and a center line is equidistant between them.

The center of the rink is marked by a blue spot in the middle of a blue circle of 457 cm (15 ft) radius. Four red spots in similar sized red circles, two in each half, are marked 457 cm (15 ft) out from the goal lines (in line with a point mid-way between the goal posts and barriers). Short lines within and beside each circle indicate where players may stand during face-offs. Creases in front of each goal are indicated by semi-circles of 182 cm (6 ft) radius (international rules) or rectangles 243 cm (8 ft) by 121 cm (4 ft) (North American rules).

For record purposes, a player who passes to the scorer of a goal is credited with an 'assist'. A goaltender who is unbeaten is credited with a 'shut-out'.

Above right: A form of foul not always intentional and sometimes difficult to avoid, called 'boarding', impeding an opponent's progress through pinning him against the barrier. This may be judged by the referee to be a major or minor penalty, depending on his assessment of the action.

Above left: A goal area meleé—but where is the puck? The action is so rapid that a referee needs an eagle eye when players get spreadeagled.

WHAT DO THEY WEAR?
Ice hockey players look big and bulky. So they may be, but their protective clothing bulk out their natural shapes in all directions.

Many players start off with long underwear to absorb perspiration during play and keep them warm if they are off the rink. Over this they wear protective pads on shoulder and chest and over the groin. Shin and elbow pads protect those vulnerable parts. All the upper padding is covered by the team shirt; the lower parts by short pants held up by braces and stockings supported by suspenders. In addition players wear helmets and gloves. Last, but not least, are their skates.

Right: A goal is saved, the puck is cleared, but could the referee see exactly how from his position? Obviously, players get away with some illegal moves on the official's blind side, but it is the very pace of the game that causes a few mix-ups and provides the keyed-up excitement for players and spectators alike.

Below: The goaltender (here a Russian) is even more protected than the rest of the team. His equipment, includes a face-protecting mask or cage, leg and body guards, a wider stick and odd gloves, one designed for holding the stick and the other for catching the puck. The rules state that the goal posts shall be painted red, and that a net of approved design is used.

TOP TEAMS

Canada has won more world and Olympic titles than any other nation and is generally considered to possess the most talented players, but Canada's true strength is not properly reflected by its team's performances in international matches because the best players are seldom available owing to club commitments.

The Soviet Union has thus dominated world championships during the past two decades and their strongest rivals have been Czechoslovakia, Sweden, Finland and U.S.

The world's best club teams and players have been largely those competing in the National Hockey League of North America, which includes both U.S. and Canadian teams.

High fences or shatterproof glass surround the rink so that the spectators are protected from a flying puck or loose hockey stick. According to the official rules it should be uniform in color, preferably white.

Above: There is clearly a foul in the center. Holding an opponent to prevent his getting to the puck—or is the front player's leg causing an obstruction?

Either way, this is the kind of balking which happens so easily in the heat of the moment at so fast a playing pace.

The players and the play

A team is made up of six people: a goaltender, two defense-men and three forwards (right and left wings and center-man). But teams may carry 17 or more players, because substitution is a key factor in match tactics. The coach decides when to replace players, and substitutions can be made whenever play stops. It is customary for a senior team to carry two goaltenders, three pairs of defenders, three forward trios and perhaps some extra utility players as well. The captain or one of the two alternative captains should always be on the rink, and can ask a referee to explain a penalty.

Ice hockey has a number of officials to oversee the rapid play. There are two referees or one referee and two linesmen, a game timekeeper, an official scorer and two goal judges. The game timekeeper records the starting and finishing time of each game and the actual playing time during the game.

Play begins with a face-off, when the referee drops the puck on the center spot between two opposing players. Play continues until the puck stops moving or goes out of the rink, or if a goal is scored or there is a penalty. Play is resumed by a face-off on the nearest of the marked spots to where a misplay occurred. When the puck hits the barrier and bounces back on to the ice, play continues. A score is indicated by a red light behind the goal concerned.

WORLD ICE HOCKEY CHAMPIONS

1920-32	Canada	1956	USSR
1933	U.S.A.	1957	Sweden
1934-35	Canada	1958-59	Canada
1936	Gt. Britain	1960	U.S.A.
1937-39	Canada	1961	Canada
1947	Czechoslovakia	1962	Sweden
1948	Canada	1963-71	USSR
1949	Czechoslovakia	1972	Czechoslovakia
1950-52	Canada	1973-75	USSR
1953	Sweden	1976-77	Czechoslovakia
1954	USSR	1978-79	USSR
1955	Canada		

OLYMPIC ICE HOCKEY CHAMPIONS

1920	Canada	1956	USSR
1924	Canada	1960	U.S.A.
1928	Canada	1964	USSR
1932	Canada	1968	USSR
1936	Gt. Britain	1972	USSR
1948	Canada	1976	USSR
1952	Canada	1980	U.S.A.

Competitive Skating

Major championship meetings normally consist of four events: men's and women's singles, pairs, and ice dancing. These have all been developed from the basic principles of skating on the edges of the blades.

There are three sections in each of the men's and women's events: compulsory figures, short free skating and long free skating.

In the compulsory figures, each competitor has to skate three figures, their tracings leaving etched indentations on the ice. Each figure is skated three times without stopping, (some of the figures are skated forwards and then backwards). The aim is to have the second and third tracings superimposed on the first.

The test is to skate the figures in good style, firmly, smoothly and surely on the edge of the blade; to turn one foot without putting the other one down; and to change the skating feet as necessary. There are 41 figures in the international schedule (each consisting of two or three lobes). The three to be skated are selected from only six of them, and these six are announced at the World Championships.

The competition events

In the short free skating, each competitor skates seven specified movements (elements), suitably linking them together within two minutes. The music is selected by the skater. The seven movements include double jumps, spins and step sequences, but the most challenging element is a named double jump combined with any double or triple jump of the skater's choice.

The long free skating requires each contestant to perform a personally created program of any number of elements, lasting five minutes for men, four for women. Level of difficulty, originality and interpretation to the skater's choice of music, all without undue repetition, are the key factors in this.

Right: Vladimir Kovalev, the Soviet skater trained by Elena Tchaikovskaia in Moscow, regained the world title in Vienna in 1979 largely because all his major rivals failed in the short free jump combination. His manner of victory was not all that inspiring and it seemed unlikely that he would enjoy so much luck again. A reliable figure tracer, but inconsistent jumper, excessively dependent on the triple cherry. Vladimir was previously world champion in 1977 and twice runner-up, in 1975 to Sergei Volkov, the only other Soviet world men's victor, and in 1976 to Britain's John Curry.

The pair skating event consists of only two sections – short free skating and long free skating.

The short program comprises six obligatory elements, suitably linked. Again, the skaters choose the music. The performance must last no more than two minutes. The elements include solo jumps and spins, a pair spin, a lift, a death spiral and a sequence of steps. The elements are announced before the season starts.

The long program lasts five minutes for each pair. They have to link together their own selection of different elements to their choice of music.

The ice dance event is divided into three sections – compulsory dances, a set-pattern dance and free dancing.

There are three compulsory dances, selected from twelve and drawn at the World Championships. Each couple has to demonstrate a technical ability to perform them in accordance with each dance's respective characteristics. Standardized music chosen by the organizers is used.

The set-pattern dance involves repeated sequences on corresponding areas of the ice. Each couple is free to interpret the dance in their own way to their choice of music, but everyone has to do so to the same specified tempo – waltz, march, quickstep, and so on. The tempo is announced before the season starts.

The free dance is the ice dance equivalent of free skating, allowing each couple to devise their own program and musical accompaniment, but the performance must be of recognizable dance character, even though it may be completely new. Changes of tempo and type of dance are allowed during the four minutes allowed for each couple.

Soon after a championship has ended, skaters begin preparing for the next. Few sports demand such diligence and dedication. Six or more hours on the ice each day is quite normal during final training.

Becoming a competition skater
Competitors are amateurs. They are not allowed to earn money through their skating ability, but their training costs are high and championship competitors often depend on subsidies.

Major Competitions

Apart from the four-yearly Olympic events, which have their own glamour appeal, the most prestigious contests in figure skating are the World championships and the European championships, both held annually. In Olympic seasons, they are still held separately and are not, as in some sports, decided concurrently with the Olympics.

European championships, for men, are one of the oldest events in international sport. They began in 1891. Events were added for women and pairs in 1930 and for ice dancing in 1954. All are now restricted to Europeans (by birth or three years' residence) though they were open to non-Europeans until 1948. All Europe's leading skaters compete each season in both the world and European events.

World championships date from 1896 for men, 1906 for women, 1908 for pairs, and 1952 for ice dancing.

All top skaters naturally compete in their own annual national championships. It is usually necessary to do this to qualify for international selection. A nation is automatically entitled to one entry in each World and European event (for which the minimum age is 12 years). Additional entries, up to a minimum of two for each nation in any event, have to be earned. These entries are based on performances in corresponding events of the previous season. If a skater finishes in the top ten, that skater's country may enter two competitors the following year. A skater finishing in the top five earns automatic entry by name the following year, providing that no nation is represented by more than three competitors in each event. Therefore, if a country had all its top three competitors finishing in the first five, they would be the most likely candidates for the following year's events. Entries for the Olympics are qualified in the same manner, but are based on the previous season's world championship performances.

Sites for world and European championships are selected by the ISU. The meetings are held in as many different countries as is practicable.

Non-championship events

In addition to the national and international championships, prominent senior skaters have a choice of international non-championship competitions to enter each year. The major annual meetings of this kind are Skate Canada, held at various Canadian sites, and the Rotary Watches Ice International, at Richmond, London. Others are held in Moscow, Vienna and Prague. Even title contenders find such contests useful to help their preparation for championships, so a big-name skater may well compete in some half-dozen major contests during a season.

The leading non-championship events are in no way obligatory to enter, but they are seldom short of willing participants of a high standard because, as in other sports, international competitions provide invaluable experience of pressure in front of large crowds. It is far better to acquire a big occasion temperament in this way than wait to be thrust into the deep end in a championship with no previous international experience. It takes several major events for most skaters to acclimatize to, and overcome, nerves caused from tension. Awareness of representing one's country and being looked to by compatriots not to let the side down can be a heavy psychological burden to bear at first. Crucial hesitation in the figures, which require utmost concentration, is the commonest reflection of nerves.

But there is necessarily a limitation on the number of events that will attract the top performers. They need to be spaced intelligently through the season, to avoid fixture clashing and to ensure that a sufficient number of the best skaters can be available without hindering their championship commitments.

Above left: Tai Babilonia and Randy Gardner in a stylish death spiral.

Left: Linda Fratianne, world champion in 1977 and 1979, has an ideal big occasion temperament. Her tiny frame belies great stamina and determination, which are proved in her admirable triple cherry combination. She paces her program shrewdly, conserving energy for those big jumps with such sure, feather-light landings.

Right: Charlie Tickner, seen here in a sit spin, reached his career peak when he captured the world crown in Ottawa in 1978. He was coached by Norma Sahlin in Denver, on a rink just a few miles from that on which his great rival, Robin Cousins, trained.

Below: Irina Rodnina and Aleksandr Zaitsev of the USSR were world pairs champions 1973–1978 and Olympic pairs champions for 1976 and 1980.

Olympic Skating

Most championship skaters consider that an Olympic gold medal is the prime award that can be won in the sport – of even more value than a world title. Skaters in the medals hunt tend to think in terms of four-year periods of preparation and although they naturally try to achieve distinction in the annual international competitions, the Winter Olympics is their major goal.

Figure skating has been on the Olympic program longer than any other sport on ice or snow. Events for men, women and pairs were first included in the 1908 Summer Games held in London. The indoor ice rink of the Prince's Skating Club, then near St. James's Park, was the site for this first Olympic skating program.

Because of the First World War, 12 years elapsed before the second series. At the Games in 1920, held in Antwerp, Belgium, ice hockey was included in the program for the first time.

The first self-contained Olympic Winter Games were held at Chamonix, in the French Alps, in 1924. The ice stadium was spectacular for its time. It had a speed skating circuit, two ice hockey rinks and areas for figure skating. It was here that men's speed skating was introduced. Women's speed skating was not included in the schedule until 1960, and ice dancing did not gain Olympic status until 1976.

Olympic skaters

The most successful Olympic figure skaters ever were the Swede, Gillis Grafström, and the Norwegian, Sonja Henie, both of whom won gold medals in three consecutive years. Grafström won his at Antwerp in 1920, at Chamonix in 1924, and at St. Moritz in 1928. Sonja Henie won gold medals at St. Moritz, Lake Placid and Garmisch in 1928, 1932 and 1936. No one since has been able to beat these records.

No pair has been able to equal this feat either, but two pairs have each won gold medals twice running: Pierre Brunet with Andrée Joly, of France, who won in 1928 and 1932, and Oleg Protopopov with Ludmila Belousova, of the USSR, who won in 1964 and 1968. Another Russian, Irina Rodnina, won three times, but with different partners.

In speed skating, until the 1980 Winter Olympics at Lake Placid, no one had won more than three events in the men's competition at one Olympic meeting. Then Eric Heiden of the U.S.A. broke all records by winning five speed skating events. In the women's events, Lydia Skovlikova, of the USSR, had in 1964 won all four events.

Right: Eric Heiden won five gold medals at Lake Placid for speed skating. This was a new Winter Olympics record. Lidia Skovlikova of the Soviet Union had won four golds in women's races at the 1964 Games at Innsbruck.

Olympic Men's Champions
1976 J Curry (Gt Britain)
1980 R Cousins (Gt Britain)

Olympic Women's Champions
1976 D. Hamill (U.S.A.)
1980 A. Pötzsch (E Germany)

Olympic Pairs Champions
1976 Zaitsev/Rodnina (USSR)
1980 Zaitsev/Rodnina (USSR)

Olympic Ice Dance Champions
1976 Gorshkov/ Pakhomova (USSR)
1980 Linichuk/Karponosov (USSR)

Right: By beating the Finnish team, the Americans carried off the gold for ice hockey for the first time in 20 years. Their great Soviet rivals took the silver.

The growth of Olympic skating

The figure skating events in the 1908 Summer Olympics in London were contested by 19 skaters, including seven women, representing six nations. When ice hockey was included in the program at the 1920 Summer Olympics in Antwerp, the total number of ice events entries was boosted to 85 (73 men and 12 women) from 10 nations. The chart on the right shows how the number of competitors has grown since those early days, and also the many different sites that have been used for the Winter Olympics.

It is expensive to install an Olympic ice stadium, and there are not many areas compact enough to stage all events on ice and snow reasonably close together. This means that future Winter Olympics may be held, on a rotation basis, at four established centers. These are likely to be Innsbruck, Lake Placid, Sapporo and Sarajevo.

The appeal of Olympic events

Olympic events have undoubtedly done a great deal to attract public attention to ice skating. Vast television audiences are now able to watch the Games, and it is in this way that many people first learn about the sport and what it involves, and become interested enough to visit their local rink.

Below: Jan Hoffman, an East German medical student, who took the silver medal in the men's figure skating at the 1980 Olympics. Robin Cousins of Britain, trailed Hoffman before the free skating finale. Then he came through with a magnificent performance, scoring seven 5.9s for artistic merit, to win the gold.

Year	Site	Men	Women	Total
	OLYMPIC WINTER GAMES COMPETITORS			
1924	Chamonix, France	280	13	293
1928	St. Moritz, Switzerland	464	27	491
1932	Lake Placid, U.S.A.	277	30	307
1936	Garmisch-Partenkirchen, Germany	680	76	756
1948	St. Moritz, Switzerland	636	77	713
1952	Oslo, Norway	624	108	732
1956	Cortina d'Ampezzo, Italy	778	146	924
1960	Squaw Valley, U.S.A.	521	144	665
1964	Innsbruck, Austria	914	197	1111
1968	Grenoble, France	1065	228	1293
1972	Sapporo, Japan	911	217	1128
1976	Innsbruck, Austria	1092	276	1368
1980	Lake Placid, U.S.A.	1012	271	1283

Below: The silver medallist in the ice dance event in the 1980 Olympics were Krisztina Regoeczy and Andras Sallay of Hungary. The Russian pair Natalia Linichuk and Gennadi Karponosov took the gold medal by a very close margin. The crowd enthusiastically backed the Hungarian pair, who said afterwards, "We won the hearts of the audience and that's the most important thing."

Ice Spectaculars

Professional show skating is consistently among the top audience ratings on television, because it is so spectacular and no technical knowledge is needed in order to enjoy it. Beauty, grace, elegance, daring, and comedy all combine with a high degree of skill to entrance the viewer.

Whether they are televised or not, most ice shows are performed in spacious arenas, to audiences averaging more than eight thousand. The shows tour major cities and towns throughout the year and this makes it worth spending a great deal of money on setting up the productions. The size and scope of the shows mean that they can have elaborate, large-scale settings, lavish costumes and imaginative, attractive lighting effects, which all contribute to their spectacular appeal.

The first ice shows

The big ice show in the form that we know it, dates from 1913, when the first one was performed by a German cast in Berlin. Its star was billed simply as Charlotte. Two years later, the same show opened in New York and Charlotte went on to become the first skating film star. Britain's first ice show opened at the London Coliseum in 1926.

The important turning point in theatrical skating came in 1936, when Sonja Henie starred in her first feature film, *One in a Million*. The permanently touring ice revue was born the same year, when *Ice Follies* opened in Tulsa, Oklahoma. *Ice Capades* began in 1940 and *Holiday on Ice* in 1944. These three companies have since operated shows continually; the first two perform mainly in North America, and *Holiday on Ice* travels all over the world.

Ice shows in North America have normally followed the revue format, while in Britain full-length musical shows have been successfully performed on ice. Notable achievements, apart from the traditional Christmas pantomimes, have been *Rose Marie, Chu Chin Chow, White Horse Inn, Snow White and the Seven Dwarfs,* and *The Dancing Years*.

Most ice stars are former amateur champions. A few outstanding performers have joined the ranks of the highest-paid performers in show business, among them Sonja Henie. Then came the Canadian, Barbara Ann Scott, who starred for two years in *Rose Marie* and Gloria Nord, an American, who, while starring in *Chu Chin Chow* at London's Wembley Arena, was chosen to skate before Queen Elizabeth II in the 1953 Royal Variety at the London Coliseum.

Ice spectaculars today

Today's skating elite, who have a far wider audience since the introduction of television spectaculars, include Peggy Fleming, Janet Lynn and Dorothy Hamill (U.S.), Karen Magnusson and Toller Cranston (Canada), and John Curry (Great Britain). Pairs have not had comparable appeal, except for the West Germans, Hans-Jürgen Bäumler and Marika Kilius.

But the major ice shows cannot thrive simply on the star appeal of ex-champions. The majority of any cast is made up of skaters who were relatively unknown as amateurs, but who have gained greater recognition as professionals because of their personality appeal and flair for showmanship. Talented supporting principals, adagio skaters, comedy acts and novelty specialists, and the well-drilled chorus lines weaving shrewdly choreographed patterns, are what add the spice and glitter to the production of these ice spectaculars.

With a vast stage and a huge audience, each usually much larger than in conventional theatre, the touring ice revue requires a constant emphasis on spectacle. This the theatrical skating impresario provides through the dramatic actions of individual artistes, an always sumptuously attired corps de ballet, lavish decor and elaborate lighting effects. This flamboyance of the ice show tradition is typified by a New Orleans jazz production number from "Holiday on Ice" (right), full of movement and colorful atmosphere.

The star performer's role combines glamour with technical expertise, completed by luxurious costumery designed to scintillate. Solo and other principal acts punctuate excerpts from top film or stage musicals, cleverly transposed to suit skating requirements. Grace and beauty give way to contrasting comedy and other novelty routines without slowing the overall tempo. American soloist Katie Walker (far right) presents her skating skills with eye-catching elegance, and French ice comedian Guy Longpré (bottom left) knows how to raise the laughs in "Holiday on Ice". Such ice revues are aimed at the masses, with the family outing particularly in mind.

Far right: The ever-elegant John Curry's concept of show skating is closer to classical ballet in style. Soon after turning professional in 1976, he began to put over his very individualistic ideas in the "John Curry Theatre of Skating", which has played resident seasons at the London Palladium, in New York and on tour.
Curry, pictured with the American, Cathy Foulkes sees skating as a very beautiful form of movement which has yet to be fully exploited in the theatre.
"On the ice", he says, "we can move in a way no one else can. I never think about skating as a sport so much as a kind of dance and a story.
"The Russians, Oleg and Ludmilla Protopopov, skated with such rare mastery that few could fail to respond to their performances on an artistic and emotional level. They inspired my ambition to explore the potential of skating as a performing art."

Glossary of Figure Skating

ARABESQUE Long sustained edge, with body bent forward from hip.

ARABESQUE SPIN (Camel spin) Executed on flat of blade, with body in arabesque position.

ARABIAN Cartwheel in the air without using arms.

AXEL Jump named after Norwegian, Axel Paulsen, begun from outside forward edge, with one-and-a-half mid-air turns, landing on back outside edge of opposite foot.

AXEL LIFT Pair move when girl, supported by man rotating beneath, turns one-and-a-half times in air. Begun from girl's outside forward edge and completed on outside back edge of opposite foot.

AXEL SIT SPIN Jump spin beginning with an axel and ending in a back sit spin.

BALLET JUMP Begun with free foot picked into the ice, then brought slightly forward with skating foot extended well back The back is arched to give a ballet pose in the air.

BRACKET Half-turn from one edge to opposite edge of the same foot.

BRACKET FIGURE Two-lobed figure with bracket turns at extreme ends, pointing away from circle centres.

BROKEN The landing of a jump where the natural rotation of the landing edge is in opposite direction to rotation of the jump.

BROKEN LEG SPIN A sit spin with the free leg extended to the side or behind the skater, with instep parallel to the ice.

BULGE Large deviation from symmetry of circle in figure.

BUNNY HOP Simple jump from one foot, landing on toe of the other, gliding back onto the jumping foot.

CAMEL SPIN (Arabesque spin) Executed on flat of blade with body in arabesque position. Name derived from original hump-back position no longer in vogue.

CHANGE FIGURE A half circle on one edge followed by a full circle on the other, in continuous movement through a change of edge.

CHANGE FOOT SIT A sit spin, changing from one foot to the other while remaining in sitting pose.

CHASSÉ A two-step sequence in which the free foot, when becoming the skating foot, does not pass the original skating foot.

CHERRY FLIP (Toe loop jump) Loop jump in which the free foot is placed behind the skating foot, with the toe on the ice before the jump.

CHOCTAW Turn where blades and direction are changed to opposite edges.

CLOSED AXEL Axel jump with free leg held close to jumping leg.

COMBINED SPIN Pair move when partners are inter-linked while spinning.

COUNTER Half-turn, entered like a bracket, exited like a three, maintaining the same edge.

CROSSFOOT SPIN Executed on the flat of both blades with legs in crossed position, toes together and heels apart.

CROSSOVER A stroke when the free foot crosses in front of the skating foot, used for forward or backward cornering.

DEATH SPIRAL Pair move, where man pivots with both knees bent, holding girl's hand while she circles round him, bending backwards until the back of her head nearly touches the ice.

DOUBLE JUMP Same as a single jump but with an extra mid-air rotation.

EDGE Either side of the blade.

FIGURE EIGHT A skating figure composed of two adjacent circles (lobes).

FLAT FOOT SPIN Simple spin on the forward part of the skate.

FLIP JUMP A toe salchow jump, assisted from the toe point of the free foot.

FLYING CAMEL Jump variation of a camel spin on a forward outside edge, with body rotating parallel to the ice, landing in a reverse camel spin.

FLYING SIT SPIN A loop jump with the body forming a sit spin pose to land in a regular sit spin.

FREE FOOT The disengaged foot opposite to the one skating a stroke.

GRAB-HOLD SPIN (or Catch parallel) Upright spin in which the free leg is raised and a hand reaches out to grab hold of the blade of the free foot.

LASSO LIFT Pair move. From a side-by-side, hand-to-hand position, the girl is lifted overhead from a forward outside take-off. With legs in split pose, she rotates one-and-a-half times while man's arm is stretched, simulating a lassoing pose.

LAY-BACK One-foot spin in which body is bent backwards.

LAY-BACK CAMEL Spin executed from a camel position, with body turned to the side.

LAY-OVER One-foot spin with body bent sideways.

LIFT Any pair move in which the man raises his partner with a continuous ascending and descending motion.

LOBE Complete circle in a figure.

LOOP Figure in which an eliptical loop is inscribed within a circle, both being skated on the same foot and on the same continuous edge.

LOOP JUMP Take-off from an outside back edge, turning once in the air, landing on the same edge of the same foot.

LUTZ Counterwise jump from back outside edge, toeing in with the free foot, with one mid-air rotation, landing on back outside edge of opposite foot.

LUTZ LIFT Pair move with counter rotation, when girl is lifted from outside back edge to the corresponding edge of the opposite foot. Each partner makes a full revolution.

MAZURKA Jump from back edge, landing on the toe of opposite foot.

MOHAWK Half-turn from one foot to the other, turning on to the corresponding edge.

OVERHEAD AXEL Pair lift, invented by a German, Ernst Baier. The partners travel forward, hand-in-hand, the girl jumping from a forward outside edge and turning one-and-a-half times over and behind her partner's head, to land on an outside back edge.

PAIR SIT SPIN While partners face each other, the man holds the girl's waist as each spins on the opposite foot. The girl's free leg extends behind and her partner's extends in front, with her skating knee between man's thighs.

PARAGRAPH FIGURE Advanced figure in which a full figure eight is performed on the same skate, instead of making a transitional change of feet at the central starting point.

PARALLEL SPIN Same as arabesque spin or camel spin.

ROCKER Turn with no change of edge.

SALCHOW Jump, invented by a Swede, Ulrich Salchow. Take-off is from an inside back edge, landing on an outside back edge of the opposite blade after an almost full mid-air turn.

SIT SPIN Invented by an American, Jackson Haines. Performed in a 'shoot-the-duck' position, with free leg extended forward and body crouched over the skating knee.

SPIRAL Any sustained move, in various positions, most commonly with body bent forward and free leg extended high behind skating leg.

SPLIT JUMP Half a mid-air rotation, with legs and arms as near horizontal to the ice as possible.

SPLIT LUTZ LIFT Pair move when girl is lifted from and landed on an outside back edge, making a lutz jump in the air.

SPREADEAGLE A sustained move with feet in line, heels together and toes pointed outwards.

STAG JUMP A half flip jump simulating the action of a deer.

THREE One-foot turn, changing direction and edge, simulating an elongated numeral three on the ice.

THREE JUMP (Waltz jump) Simple jump entailing a half-turn in the air, taking off from a forward outside edge and landing on the back outside edge of the other foot.

THROW AXEL Pair move achieved by throwing the lifted girl through the air from the force of the man's axel jump.

THROW SALCHOW Pair move in which girl is thrown from force of the man's salchow jump.

TRACING The marks made on the ice by a skate blade.

TRIPLE JUMP Same as a single jump, but with two extra mid-air rotations.

TWIST LIFT Pair move involving one or more mid-air rotations by the girl during descent.

TWIZZLE Dance move involving a complete 180 degrees rotation of the skating blade, almost on one spot.

WALLEY Named after Nathan Walley. The only reverse jump apart from the lutz, taking off from a back inside edge with a clockwise mid-air rotation before landing on the back outside edge of the same foot.

Index

ACKNOWLEDGEMENTS

Design: David Nash

Illustrations: David Nash, Thelma Bissex

Picture research: Penny J. Warn and Tracey Rawlings

Cover: All Sport (Tony Duffy)

Endpapers: All Sport (Tony Duffy)

Illustrations in text:
All Sport (Tony Duffy): page 7;
page 8; page 20 bottom;
page 21; page 23; page 24;
page 25; page 26 left;
page 27 right; page 28 top;
page 29; page 31 bottom;
page 32; page 33;
page 34 bottom; page 35;
page 36 bottom; page 38 top.
All Sport (Don Morley): page 4;
page 6 top; page 22; page 37.
Allsport (Steve Powell):
page 15 bottom left;
Camera Press London: page 43 bottom.
Colorsport: page 6 bottom;
page 14 bottom right;
page 27 left; page 34 top;
page 36 top.
Daily Telegraph: page 45.
E. D. Lacey: page 28 bottom;
page 38 bottom.
Fotopersbureau: page 9;
page 30; page 31 top.
International Holiday on Ice:
page 42; page 43 top.
Kobal Collection: page 11.
National Gallery (London):
page 6 right; page 10 top.
Mansell Collection: Page 10 bottom.
Sporting Pictures: page 13;
page 20 top; page 26 right;
page 39 right.
Van Cleve Photography
(David Lissy): page 39 left.

Editor: Deborah Manley

Adviser: David Clements

Left: John Curry, even when caught unawares by the camera during a rehearsal, is still seen to be the earnest perfectionist. Note the concentration on his face and the perfect poise in a graceful, forward-leaning arabesque position, with the toe of the straightened non-skating leg elegantly pointed.